FOR
EVERY
ONE

JASON REYNOLDS

For You.

For Me.

KNIGHTS OF
Published by the Knights Of
Knights Of Ltd, Registered Offices: 119 Marylebone Road,
London, NW1 5PU

www.knightsof.media
First published 2018
001

Written by Jason Reynolds
Text and cover copyright © Jason Reynolds, 2018
Cover art by © Yinka Illori, 2018
First published in the USA by Atheneum,
an imprint of Simon and Schuster, Inc, 2018
All rights reserved
The moral right of the author and illustrator has been asserted

Set in 12pt Ovo Regular
Design and Typeset by Marssaié Jordan
Printed and bound in the UK

A CIP catalogue record for this book will be available from the British
Library

ISBN: PB: 978-1-9996425-3-2
2 4 6 8 10 9 7 5 3 1

FOR
EVERY
ONE

JASON REYNOLDS

A NOTE:

When I started writing this, I didn't know what it was. A poem in form only, a letter written in parts, an offering that I've now been working on for years.

A thing.

But when I think of it now, and the process of it all, I realize that it was basically just the undoing of . . . me—a twenty-something clinging tight to the nugget of thin air I referred to as my dream. And as the meltdown happened, I realized that many of the people around me were melting as well. My friends who stayed up all night with me in Brooklyn—painting, and playing music, writing, practicing and pushing—were growing tired and annoyed, frustrated with the uncertainty. People in my family, the "responsibles," whom I argued and disagreed with, never knew that I could see that the remnants of this same kind of meltdown that may have happened to them forty years prior were still there, hiding beneath their tongues.

And for some reason, around this time I also met quite a few teenagers who carried with them an unfortunate practicality. It was as if their imaginations had been seat belted, kept safe from accidents. Sure, they still had adolescent gusto, but only in speech. When asked about their dreams and passions, though, many could only answer halfway. They could admit that the dreams were real and that there were things they wanted to do, say, see, and make, but they couldn't get past how foolish it is to be foolish.

And I couldn't blame them. Any of them. I had tried to do something different, and it was killing me. And my friends. And my family. But the dream was still there, still painfully undeniable.

So, I started writing this. A letter to myself to keep from quitting. It was written while I was afraid. Unsure. Doubtful. And at first, I wasn't sure what it was. A poem in form only, a letter written in parts, an offering, that I've now been working on for years.

For me, a mighty, mighty thing.

*"Though we do not wholly believe it yet,
the interior life is a real life,
and the intangible dreams of people
have a tangible effect on the world."*
—*James Baldwin*

01

DEAR
DREAMER,

THIS LETTER IS BEING WRITTEN

from a place of raw honesty and love

but not at all

a place of expertise

on how to make

your dreams come true.

I DON'T KNOW NOTHING

ABOUT THAT.

I HAVEN'T GONE THROUGH IT ALL

and come out on the other side

pinned with a

blue ribbon,

draped in

a victor's sash

or dollar bills

or even unshakable happiness.

IN FACT,

I have yet to see
my own dream
made tangible.

THIS LETTER
IS BEING WRITTEN
FROM THE INSIDE.

From the front line
and the fault line.
From the uncertain thick of it all.
From a man with a
straight-line mouth
and an ego
with a slow leak.

From a man doing it
the only way
he knows how,
splitting his cries
and his smiles
right down the middle,
swallowing his moonshine mistakes
while in the sunlight his sweat
irrigates his life and that life he—
like you—

HAS BEEN TILLING, HOPING

THERE'S A HARVEST COMING.

AT SIXTEEN I thought

I would've made it by now.
At eighteen I said twenty-five
is when I'd make my first million.
At twenty-five I moved back in
with my mother,
bill collectors
breathing on me like
Brooklyn summer.

And now at
ALMOST TWENTY-EIGHT

I'm just
ALMOST TWENTY-EIGHT

SO I GOT NO ANSWERS

THE TRUTH IS

our dreams could be
as far away as forever
or as close as lunchtime.

Tomorrow you could
wake up and read
this letter on a billboard.

Or you could wake up
and have forgotten
who wrote it.

IT ALL JUST DEPENDS.

Some say on skill.

Some say on will.

Some say on luck.

Some say on buck.

Some say on race.

Some say on face.

Some say on Sunday

God got a mighty,
mighty plan.

Nobody really knows
what it depends on,
but everybody knows

IT DEPENDS.

SO I WENT OUT

and bought all the books
on all the ways to make
dreams come true,
laying out the how-to,
somehow spinning life
into a fantastic formula
for dummies and
dream chasers,
written by experts and
dream catchers

who swear that I
can one plus one
and right foot
left foot
my way into fulfillment,

never taking into
consideration
all this mess I got
strapped to my
back and my head
and my legs and

MY HEART.

And them books
didn't bandage my
fattened flat feet,
swollen from
this journey.
The pages
didn't spend
nor could they
be eaten to ease
the hunger.

Though I could
curl up with one,
I couldn't curl up
on one
and get a
decent rest
or a respite from
the hunt.

USELESS.

I thought about
burning them.

At least
I could use the
firelight for this

LONG AND OFTEN

DARK ROAD.

ONE THING
I AM NOW CERTAIN OF

is that this

road less traveled has

in fact

been traveled by more suckers

than you think.

All of us out here,

slumped over wearing

weird fake

broken smiles,

trying to avoid the truth:

THAT WE ALL GOT

ROAD RAGE.

WE ARE a bunch of
exhausted stragglers,
exalted strugglers,
disciples of the dreamers who
came before us.
Students of a
different bible,
reading the book
of the City of Angels
and the Big Apple,

an orange house in
old New Orleans,
a cheap barren flat
above a bistro
in Paris.

We are led by the Moses in our minds
to the Promised Land
in our hearts
we know is real.

AT SIXTEEN

I thought
I would've made it
by now.

NOW

I'm making up
what making it
means

ASIGO.

But this letter
is not about making it,

because I don't know nothing about that.

I don't know nothing about that

at all.

02

WHAT I DO KNOW

is how it feels.

How it feels
when that spirit thing
won't stop
raking the metal mug
across your rib cage,
clanging
like a machine gun
fired at a church bell,
vibrating everything
irreverent inside.

Sounds like a prison
revolt
that only you
can hear
and feel.

And nasty things
are being said
about the prison guard—

that scared
controlling
oppressive part
of you

AND EVERYONE ELSE.

If you are
anything like me,
you hope
it never stops.
You hope the
bubbling never
dies down
and the yearning to
break out and
break through
never simmers.

YOU HOPE

the voice that
delivers the
loudest whispers
of what you envision never silences.
That it never cowers behind fear
and expectations that other people
strap to your life
like a backpack full of bricks
(or books written by
experts).

Because if it did—
if it disappeared,
if the voices vanished
and you were no longer
overtaken by the
taunts of your own
potential,
no longer blinded
by a perfect vision
of your purpose,
no longer engorged
with passion—
what would happen?

WELL,
I GUESS
NOTHING.

And to me,
there is
NOTHING SCARIER
than
NOTHING.

Even when nothing seems
to be going right

or Nothing seems to be
going right.

I'd rather be bothered
by the loud knocking
on the door inside.

Even though I answered
years ago,
the knocking continues.

I'd rather my appetite

be whet by a teaspoon

of almost-there

every now and then.

I'd rather suffer from
internal eczema,
constantly irritated
by the itch of possibility.

There have been
many anxious nights
where darkness
has slept around me,

my friends
cocooned in a
coziness I have
yet to meet.

My eyes
swollen with exhaustion,
my body sputtering
on its way down,

but my dream
won't stop crying,
screaming
like a colicky
infant.

Sometimes I think
it needs to be changed.

USUALLY
IT JUST NEEDS TO BE FED.

So I feed it everything
I have.

And
it feeds me everything
I have.

Though the struggle
is always made to
sound admirable
and poetic,
the thumping uncertainty
is still there.

SURE,

I know my dream

is as real

as my hands

but I grip tight
a short leash
with insecurity
tied to the end

wagging along
beside me.

If you're like me,
you've struggled trying
to stomp out
the flame of doubt
and fear,
the warmth and comfort
always enticing
and familiar
though venomous
and life extinguishing.

I KNOW PEOPLE WHO

have burned.
A burn so violent
it can't be categorized
by any numbered degree.

I know people who
have burned
from foot
to torso
emotionally.

Legs of passion
turned to soot.

Yet no matter how
hard I've tried
to escape it,
to kill the
deceptive heat
dancing like a
devil's tongue,
to douse it with all
the will and faith
I can muster,
I know
a tiny ember
always glows
beneath the brush.

It whispers to me
only when I step to
the edge of excellence.

My toes clawing
the cliff,
my mind already airborne.

It whispers to me
that I don't have wings
that I don't have a shot
that I don't have a clue
but to me,

I don't have a choice,
so I jump
anyway.

Dreamer,
if you are like me,

YOU
    JUMP
        ANYWAY.

03

THIS LETTER ISN'T

for any specific
kind of dream.
It isn't intended
for a certain genre,
medium,
trade, or
denomination.

It is only intended
FOR THE COURAGEOUS.

Maybe you are a dancer

moving to the sound of your own future;

or a musician

banging strumming bowing plucking

blowing into,

creating soundtracks

for dream trains chugging along

through thick night;

or a painter
spilling and splattering confessions
across the face of stretched canvas;
or an actor
praying at the altar
of your alter ego;
or a photographer,
finger on the button
like a quick-draw cowboy,
shooting
not to kill anyone
but to preserve forever;

or maybe even
a writer
for some strange reason,
writing expert books,
pages of good intention
and rah-rah and fantasy
and sometimes truth,
or maybe even letters to people
you don't know but
do know you love.

Or maybe you aren't
an artist at all.

DREAMS AREN'T RESERVED FOR THE CREATIVES.

Maybe you're an athlete,
a gladiator hoping for
a shot at the lion.
Maybe you're eighteen
and plan to make your first million
by twenty-five
(it's not impossible).
Or maybe you're eighteen
and plan to make it to twenty-one
(it's not impossible, nor is
twenty-two twenty-three twenty-four).

At twenty-five I moved back in with my
mother
and found out
she loved to teach
little kids,
and bake,
and help the needy—
her passion made plain,
her dream made real
after forty years
of forty hours a week
behind a desk.
You might be fifty
and think it's too late.

JUMP ANYWAY.

Dreams don't have timelines,
deadlines,
and aren't always in
straight lines.

JUMP ANYWAY.

OR MAYBE

your dream is to have a family,
to wear corny T-shirts
and hold up signs
and be the cameraman
at the little one's
games.

To kiss your child
on head and heart,
selflessly fertilizing
his or her passion.
Stay awake with them
when the dream
is crying
like a colicky infant;

help them feed it
and before sleep
do your best to
smother
that tiny ember
of doubt and fear
that glows
beneath the brush.

THIS LETTER
IS FOR
US ALL.

The awkward angels
with crooked halos and
second-hand wings.
The irresponsible
and curious
fire-bellied babies.
The deformed, with
hearts on the outside
and ears on the inside.
The squares who
use nine-to-five cubes
as planning sessions
for the real work.

For the rebel children,
the wild ones
the long-shots
the bad-mouthed
the side-eyed
the terribly terribly
terribly envied
secretly
by the safe.
For those who bear the cross—
the two perpendicular
planks of passion—
who find life is best
when nailed to it.

For the jumpers.

For the jumpers.

For the jumpers.

THIS LETTER
IS FOR US ALL,

to remind us

that we are many.

That we are right

for trying.

That purpose is real.

That making it is possible.

But this letter

is not about making it,

BECAUSE I DON'T KNOW NOTHING ABOUT THAT.

I DON'T KNOW NOTHING ABOUT THAT

at all.

Besides,

I'm not sure

making it

even matters

so much.

04

When it comes to
my dream,
the way I like to describe it
is that
it's a rabid beast
that found me when I
was young.

It bit me
and infected me,
but before
I could catch it,
it shot off into
the darkness.
Now I spend my life
searching for it,
hunting it down.

I know I'm on its trail.

I can smell it.

I can hear it.

SOMETIMES I THINK I CAN EVEN SEE IT.

EITHER WAY,

I know
I'm on the right track—
my nose to the dirt,
foaming at the spirit.
I look under heavy stones,
behind massive trees,
deep in dark caves,
and I will keep looking
until I find that beast,
that thing that bit me
when I was young.

THE TRUTH IS,

finding that beast may
or may not happen.
But the treasures I've discovered under the
heavy stones
and behind the massive trees
and deep in the dark caves
have created the hunter
and the human
that I am.

Your dream is the mole
behind your ear,
that chip in your
front tooth,
your freckles.

It's the thing that makes
you special,
but not the thing that makes
you great.

The courage in trying,
the passion in living,
and the acknowledgment
and appreciation of
the beauty happening around
you does that.

DREA

MER,

I am not fit to say much more,
because I don't know much more than
that.
If you do,
please write back.
If not,
please accept this
as just a few words
of encouragement.
And if this letter means nothing to you,
if it's just more pointless weight
added to an already heavy life,
feel free to burn it
and use it for firelight
for this
long and often dark
road.

But if you somehow find truth,
comfort,
or anything at all
within this ramble,
keep it close
and use it for firelight
for this
long and often dark
road.

With love,
Jason Reynolds